Wardfold, Deeside
July 1983

F...
hope ...   d
many ...
the ...   ...
                          vid

TIME

Also by Yehuda Amichai

AMEN

SONGS OF JERUSALEM AND MYSELF

POEMS

NOT OF THIS TIME, NOT OF THIS PLACE

TIME

Poems by Yehuda Amichai

HARPER & ROW, PUBLISHERS
New York, Hagerstown,
San Francisco, London

TIME. Copyright © 1979 by Yehuda Amichai. All rights reserved. Printed in the United States of America. No part of this book may be used or reproduced in any manner whatsoever without written permission except in the case of brief quotations embodied in critical articles and reviews. For information address Harper & Row, Publishers, Inc., 10 East 53rd Street, New York, N.Y. 10022. Published simultaneously in Canada by Fitzhenry & Whiteside Limited, Toronto.

FIRST EDITION

Designed by Janice Stern

Library of Congress Cataloging in Publication Data
  Amichai, Yehuda.
    Time.
    I. Title.
  PJ5054.A65T5 1979   892.4'1'6   78-66388
  ISBN 0-06-010088-5

---

79 80 81 82 83 10 9 8 7 6 5 4 3 2 1

CONTENTS

1. "Songs of continuity, land mines and graves."   1
2. "At the monastery of Latroun"   2
3. "On this evening"   3
4. "My son was born in a hospital called Assuta."   4
5. "The bodies of two lovers hurt"   5
6. "The soldiers in the grave"   6
7. "In each buying and each loving"   7
8. "This is my mother's house."   9
9. "What's this?"   11
10. "No eye has ever seen"   12
11. "How beautiful are thy tents, Jacob."   13
12. "Advice for good love"   14
13. "Shifra and Batia promised"   15
14. "This girl, halfway through high school"   16
15. "I passed a house where I once lived"   17
16. "People on this shore"   18
17. "To my love, while combing her hair"   19
18. "'One sees all kinds of things'"   20

19. "How did a flag come into being?"   21

20. "The diameter of the bomb was thirty centimeters"   22

21. "The figure of a Jewish father I am"   23

22. "What's that?"   24

23. "Sons of warm wombs join the army."   25

24. "When my head got banged on the door, I screamed"   26

25. "'Sometime before his death'"   27

26. "This garden with your confession in it"   28

27. "The old ice factory in Petah-Tikvah"   29

28. "I heard talking outside my window"   30

29. "I've filtered out of the Book of Esther the residue"   31

30. "My friend, the things you do now"   32

31. "I've already been weaned from Adam's, the first man's, curse."   33

32. "When I was young the land was young"   34

33. "Listen, my old teacher"   36

34. "The door opened by mistake"   37

35. "In the garden at the white table"   38

36. "I'm like a leaf"   39

37. "Karl Marx, cold and bitter one"   40

38. "A weeping mouth and a laughing mouth"   42

39. "My child dreamt about me in his sleep"   43
40. "'But what have you done for your soul?'"   44
41. "The evening lies along the horizon and donates blood."   45
42. "These words, like heaps of feathers"   46
43. "A song, a psalm, on Independence Day."   47
44. "The little park planted in memory of a boy"   48
45. "On New Year's Day, next to a house being built"   49
46. "You carry the load of heavy buttocks"   51
47. "In the beginning there was great joy"   52
48. "There came upon me a terrible longing"   53
49. "I am a man 'planted beside streams of water'"   54
50. "A song of friendship, while parting from a friend"   55
51. "To a friend who is a priest"   56
52. "Jerusalem is a cradle city rocking me."   58
53. "At an archeological site"   59
54. "Evening hours of the soul"   60
55. "A snare flies up from the ground"   61
56. "In Talpiot the floors are slowly sinking."   62
57. "The cemetery of Messilat Zion in the mountains"   63
58. "This man crossing the field"   64
59. "Early in the morning"   65

60. "The day olive trees breathed deeply" 66
61. "With open eyes as only the dead have" 67
62. "Departure from a place where you had no love" 68
63. "When a man has been away from his homeland a long time" 69
64. "I love these people in their strong house" 70
65. "The house, in which I had many thoughts" 71
66. "Late in life I came to you" 72
67. "We walked together, you and I" 73
68. "Small and fragile you stand in the rain" 74
69. "My son, in whose face there is already a sign" 75
70. "In this valley" 76
71. "'He left two sons'" 77
72. "My ex-pupil has become a policewoman." 78
73. "Such a male on a bald mountain in Jerusalem" 79
74. "So I find myself always on the run" 80
75. "A bird at dawn is singing" 82
76. "On the wall of a house" 83
77. "My God, the soul you gave me" 84
78. "Here on the ancient beach of Tantura I sit" 85
79. "Now all the lifeguards have left for their homes." 86
80. "So I went down to the ancient harbor" 88

1

Songs of continuity, land mines and graves.
These are turned up when you build a house or a road:
Then come the black crow people from Meah Sh'earim*
to screech bitterly "dead, dead." Then come
young soldiers and with hands still bare from last night
they dismantle iron and decipher death.

So come, let's build no house and pave no road!
Let's make a house folded up in the heart
and a road rolled up in a coil in the soul, inside,
and we shall not die forever.

People here live inside prophecies that came true
as inside a thick cloud after an explosion
that did not disperse.
And so in their lonely blindness they
touch each other between the legs, in the twilight,
for they have no other time and they
have no other place,
and the prophets died long ago.

---

* Meah Sh'earim—Quarter of the ultra-orthodox in Jerusalem.

2

At the monastery of Latroun, in expectation of wine
being wrapped for me in the cool house,
there fell upon me all the laziness
of this land: holy, holy, holy.

I lay in the dry grass, on my back,
I saw high summer clouds in the sky,
motionless, like me below.
Rain in another land, peace in my heart.
And from my penis white seeds will fly
as from a dandelion tuft.
(Come, blow: poof, poof.)

3

On this evening I think again
about many days
that have sacrificed themselves
for just one night of love.
I think about this waste and this waste's fruit,
about abundance and about fire
and how without pain—time.

I've seen roads leading from one man
to another woman.
I've seen a life blurred
like a letter in the rain.
I've seen a dining table on which
things were left,
and wine on which was written, "The Brothers,"
and how without pain—time.

4

My son was born in a hospital called Assuta.*
Since then I have watched
his life as much as I could.

My son, when schools leave you
and you are left bare and vulnerable,
when you see life being torn
at its edges, and the world
falling apart at the joints, come again to me:
I'm still a great expert
on bewilderment and calm.

I'm like a peaceful album
with its photographs torn out
or just fallen out by themselves.
It has lost almost nothing of its weight.
So I have stayed the same man,
almost without memories.

* Assuta—a hospital in Tel-Aviv.

5

The bodies of two lovers hurt
after rolling all day long in the grass.

Their lying-awake-together at night
brings salvation to the world,
but not to them.

A bonfire burning in the open field
repeats blind with pain
the sun's work during the day.

Childhood is far away.
War is near. Amen.

6

The soldiers in the grave say: You above
who place wreaths on us,
like a life preserver made of flowers,
regard our faces so alike
between the outstretched arms. But
remember the difference there was between us
and the joy on the surface of the water.

7

In each buying and each loving
something has remained of our
Father Abraham's biblical wisdom,
when he bought a beautiful and cool
cave-tomb, while still alive,
to stay forever and remember.
That's the way to love in this land
and that's the way to buy.

And on Lag Be'omer* people get
married and make bonfires.
The smell of burning is in the air
together with the perfume of brides.
Rabbis carry folded wedding canopies
on their shoulders like stretchers
to be used again and again
on this day.

And children carry bows and arrows
to play until it's a real war.
That's the way to fight wars.

And that's the way to remember in this land,
in which childhoods are far away from people
like times before the destruction of the temple.

* Lag Be'omer—a memorial day in summer on which bonfires and many weddings are held.

They have a "Book of Children, One"
and a "Book of Children, Two"
like the "Book of Kings, One" and the
"Book of Kings, Two" in the Bible.

8

This is my mother's house. The plant
which started to climb on it
in my childhood has grown since and
clings to its wall. But I was
torn away long ago.

Mother, in pain you gave birth to me,
in pain lives your son.
His sadness is combed and groomed,
his happiness well dressed.
With his dream he earns his bread
and with his bread his dream.
The average annual rainfall
does not touch him
and degrees of temperature will
pass by him in weeping shade.

Oh my mother, who presented
me with a first welcome drink
in this world: L'haim, l'haim,*
my son!
I haven't forgotten a thing, but my life
has become calm and deep
like a second gulp deep in the throat,
not like the first one, with sucking
smacking, happy lips.

* L'haim—"To your health!" in Hebrew.

Your steps on the stairs
have always stayed in me,
never coming nearer and never going away,
like heartbeats.

9

What's this? This is an old
toolshed.
No, this is a great past love.

Anxiety and Joy were here together
in this darkness
and Hope.
Perhaps I've been here once before.
I didn't go near to find out.

These are voices calling out of a dream.
No, this is a great love.
No, this is an old toolshed.

10

No eye has ever seen,
nor any ear heard,
no bird has ever told it:
This child, sleeping, like a compass needle
trembling slightly at night.
But his head doesn't
move, secure in the holy ark
of his father's worry.

No eye has ever seen,
no dream ever dreamt
no mouth ever spoken this child.

In ancient times they used to say:
"Loved, like the apple of his eye." What, what,
like the apple of his eye? This child.
What is the apple of an eye? A ball made
from tears and paint.

Oh, all my words, sad
and happy nails of my life.

11

"How beautiful are thy tents, Jacob."
Even now, when there are neither tents nor Jacob's
tribes, I say, how beautiful.

Oh, may there come something of redemption,
an old song, a white letter,
a face in the crowd, a door opening
for the eye, multicolored
ice cream for the throat,
oil for the guts, a warm
memory for the breast.

Then my mouth will open wide
in everlasting praise,
open like the belly of a
wide-open calf hung on a hook
in a butcher's shop of the Old City market.

12

Advice for good love: Don't love
those from far away. Take yourself one
from nearby.
The way a sensible house will take
local stones for its building,
stones which have suffered in the same cold
and were scorched by the same sun.
Take the one with the golden wreath
around her dark eye's pupil, she
who has a certain knowledge
about your death. Love also inside
ruins like taking honey out of
the lion's carcass that Samson killed.

And advice for bad love: With
the love left over
from the previous one
make a new woman for yourself,
then with what is left of that woman
make again a new love,
and go on like that
until nothing remains for you.

13

Shifra and Batia promised
with their hips eternal youth.

Their dates of birth, still so fresh,
fill their thighs with sweet tension
and my brain with a golden sound like a light
 string.

They said: Aren't men weird and crazy
to decorate a sword made to kill
with beautiful carvings and precious stones,
but the penis, which is all made for joy,
they don't decorate.

14

This girl, halfway through high school,
brings back to me lost things
without knowing it herself.
I don't know her name, but
she is so beautiful that I feel happy
not to be her father, and not her god.

Will we still love her even
when they cut away from her body
a leg or a hand, an ear or the nose?

Her belly is still a soft botanical belly
not hard like bellies of man-eating evil women.
Her eyes are clear without mist of generations.
In her smooth hair there still remains
like some imprint of a wreath of flowers
a memory from a harvest dance in school
in her childhood.

Will we still love her
when they chop off
more and more
until nothing is left of her
but a basketful of girl,
a basketful of you?

15

I passed a house where I once lived:
A man and a woman are still together in the whispers.
Many years have passed with the silent buzz
of staircase bulbs—on, off, on.

The keyholes are like small delicate wounds
through which all the blood has oozed out
and inside people are pale as death.

I want to stand once more as in my
first love, leaning on the doorpost
embracing you all night through, standing.
When we left at early dusk the house
started to crumble and collapse
and since then the town
and since then the whole world.

I want once more to have this longing
until dark red burn marks show in the skin.

I want once more to be written
in the book of life, to be written
anew every day
until the writing hand hurts.

16

People on this shore will never again
step into the footprints which
they left in the sand
while last passing here.

This is a weeping truth
but sometimes it weeps
out of happiness
about the world being so wide
that there is no need to come back
to the same places.
Everything is up in heaven.

Toward evening I saw
a tanned lifeguard
bending over a golden rescued woman
reviving her with his breath,
like lovers.

17

To my love, while combing her hair
without a mirror, facing me,
a psalm: You've washed your hair
with shampoo: A whole pine forest
breathes on your head in nostalgia.

Calmness from inside and calmness from outside
have hammered your face
between them like copper.

The pillow on your bed is your auxiliary brain
folded under your neck for memory and dream.

The earth trembles beneath us, my love.
Let's lie together, a double safety lock.

18

"One sees all kinds of things," said the Swedish
officer observing at the armistice line.
"All kinds of things," and said nothing more.

"One sees a lot of things," said the old
shoeshine man by the Jaffa gate
when a Swedish girl in a very short dress
stood above him, without looking at him
with her proud eyes.

The prophet who looked into the opening heaven saw,
and so did God, "all kinds of things" down there
   beyond the smoke,
and the surgeon saw when he cut open a cancerous
   belly
and closed it again.

"One sees all kinds of things," said
our ancestor Jacob on his bed after the blessing
which took his last strength. "All kinds
of things," and he turned
toward the wall and he died.

19

How did a flag come into being?
Let's assume that in the beginning
there was something whole, which was
then torn into two pieces, both big enough
for two battling armies.

Or like the ragged striped fabric
of a beach chair in an abandoned
little garden of my childhood,
flapping in the wind. This
too could be a flag making you arise
to follow it or to weep at its side,
to betray it or to forget.

I don't know. In my wars
no flag-bearer marched in front
of the gray soldiers in clouds of dust and smoke.
I've seen things starting as spring,
ending up with hasty retreat
in pale dunes.
I'm now far away from all that, like one
who in the middle of a bridge
forgets both its ends
and remains standing there
bent over the railing
to look down into the streaming water:
This too is a flag.

20

The diameter of the bomb was thirty centimeters
and the diameter of its effective
range—about seven meters.
And in it four dead and eleven wounded.
And around them in a greater circle
of pain and time are scattered
two hospitals and one cemetery.
But the young woman who was
buried where she came from
over a hundred kilometers away
enlarges the circle greatly.
And the lone man who weeps over her death
in a far corner of a distant country
includes the whole world in the circle.
And I won't speak at all about the crying of orphans
that reaches to the seat of God
and from there onward, making
the circle without end and without God.

21

The figure of a Jewish father I am
with a sack on my back returning
home from the market. I have a rifle hidden
among soft woman-things in the closet in the scent
 of lingerie.
A man hit by the past and ill with future I am.
The fever of the present in his reddened eyes
unpaid and in vain he stands guard against evil.
Useless he guards against death,
guarding Jewish flesh, sweet like
all hunted flesh in agony. And at evening
he hears church bells rejoicing at the plight of Jews.
And from the hills a sad maneuver of brigades
with guns that have roots instead of wheels.
And he buys himself cream
for his cracked boots and his cracked lips.
And he smears it on for healing and for peace.

And he has documents of mercy and
papers of love in his coat.
And he sees people in their haste hurrying from past
 into future.
And at night, lonely and slowly he cooks jam,
stirring round and round till it grows pulpy and dense
with thick bubbles like thick Jewish eyes
and froth, white and sweet for coming generations.

22

What's that? That's an airplane at
daybreak. No, they are digging a sewer
up there. No, this is a deep
rift running along this wonderful nightingale.
No, this is a violent tearing sexual orgy
between a male and a female bulldozer.
No, this is the screech of a peacock:
This beautiful bird utters such a bitter scream.
But this is a silent song of praise.
No, these are words of comfort
for mourners, humming like
a kettle on a dying fire. But
this, surely, was an explosion!
No, this was a hollow and very heavy nightingale.
This sounds like night. No, this
was a lark announcing the new day.
This is the sunrise of nations.
No, this is my friend, the quiet cannonier,
whistling and feeding his domestic cannons
with shells at early dawn.

What's this? This is a misunderstanding of love:
Don't be frightened, child, this dog
loves you. He only wants to play with you.
Just a misunderstanding of love,
like our tears at the old window
overlooking the valley.

23

Sons of warm wombs join the army.
Those with feet kissed by mothers and aunts
and with shoes decorated with buckles and
 beautiful buttons
will have to pass through minefields.

Their eyelashes, glory of their beauty,
will become a double fence,
letting no one in and no one out.

Oh, what bar-mitzvahs* will they have,
what good deeds, what wedding parties!

Therefore, mothers, make round sons
round without hard joints,
make them like balls
that won't get hurt, just bounce
and bounce and bounce.

---

* bar mitzvah—Jewish confirmation of boys at the age of 13.

24

When my head got banged on the door, I screamed,
"My head, my head." And I screamed, "Door, door."
And I did not scream, "Mother," and not, "God."
Nor did I speak of the vision of the End of Days
of a world where there will be no heads and doors
 anymore.

When you stroked my head I whispered,
"My head, my head," and I whispered, "Your hand, your
 hand."
And I did not whisper, "Mother," and not, "God."
And I did not see wonderful visions
of hands stroking heads in the wide-opening heavens.

Whatever I scream and speak and whisper is
to comfort myself: My head, my head.
Door, door. Your hand, your hand.

25

"Sometime before his death," that's
what I overheard once while
passing two people standing at the traffic light.

As when someone leaves you
and enters into a dream
never to come out again.

Or when you put out
the lights of a big chandelier
with many bulbs
and you have to switch off all of them
and then go once more through all the stages
of light:
small light, big light,
and only after that, darkness.

26

This garden with your confession in it:
"Destroyed by love," you said
and other things which I've forgotten.

But I remember the tops of the trees
already darkening above
while the words below were still in light.

And there is a window
and he who opened it
will never be the one to close it.

And there is a number
on the door of a house
which was marked into my heart
like a number branded into a horse's skin.

"Destroyed by love." And other last
voices which have since
become food for birds and little animals of night.

27

The old ice factory in Petah-Tikvah:*
a wooden tower, boards blackened by rot.
In my childhood a weeping lived there.
I remember the tears
dripping from board to board
to still the summer's rage
and make ice below
which slid out of a deep opening.

And immediately, behind the dark cypresses,
they started to talk! "You live
only once."

I didn't understand then
and now that I understand, it's too late.

The cypresses are just as they were
and the water goes on
dripping somewhere else.

---

* Petah-Tikvah—old village in Israel.

28

I heard talking outside my window:
A woman like a dove, a dove, a dove.
So I said in my heart: My two sons
are so far from each other, so far
in time, in place, and in mother.

My world is all mixed up: The tears
astray in my throat, my ear, my nose.

There, on that balcony, I was once loved.
Now the plants have grown and cover it all.

I'm outside. I'm a clock-hand
which has run away from its clock
but cannot forget its circling movement.

When I go straight toward my endless end
it hurts, because I only know how to go round.

29

I've filtered out of the Book of Esther the residue
of vulgar joy, and out of the Book of Jeremiah
the howl of pain in the guts. And out of the
Song of Songs the endless search for love,
and out of the Book of Genesis the dreams
and Cain, and out of Ecclesiastes
the despair and out of the Book of Job—Job.
And from what was left over I pasted for myself a new
    Bible.
Now I live censored and pasted and limited and in peace.

A woman asked me last night in the darkened street
about the well-being of another woman
who had died before her time, and not in anyone's time.
Out of great tiredness I answered her:
She's fine, she's fine.

30

My friend, the things you do now
some years ago, I did.
The number of years I'm older than you
is the time that has passed since.

You can see me now, hard-eyed and soft-necked.
My penis is the last bridgehead
thrust into a new generation of young women.

After this comes the removal
of love's remnants and rubbish of joy
like that of any annoying and hampering garbage.

I can see you grasping
desperately at all that surrounds you,
books, children, a woman,
musical instruments—
but you don't know that this
is nothing but pulling
dry twigs and dead branches to your body
for the big fire
in which you'll burn.

31

I've already been weaned from Adam's, the first man's,
 curse.
The twisting fiery sword is far away,
blazing in the sun like a propellor.
I already love the salty taste of the sweat of my brow
on my bread, together with dust and death.

But still the soul I was given
is like a tongue
that remembers sweet tastes.

I am already the second man. And they are already
chasing me out of the garden of curses
in which I settled down after the garden of Eden.

Now beneath my feet there grows for me
a small cave, fitted perfectly to the shape of my body.
I am a man of shelter: the Third Man.

32

When I was young the land was young
and my own father was everyone's father.
When I was happy the land was happy too.
And when I jumped on the ground, the ground
jumped under my feet. And the grass that covered it
  in spring
softened me too. Its dry hard soil in summer
hurt the cracked skin of my own feet.
When I had my great love
they declared my land's liberation.
When my hair flew in the wind, so did its flags.
When I fought, it had wars.
When I rose, it rose up. And when
I sank it started sinking with me.

Now I come apart from all this
like something that was glued, when the glue dries out.
I detach myself and curl into myself.

Not long ago I saw a clarinet player
in the Police Band, playing at the Tower of David.
His hair was white, his face peaceful.
The face of 1946—that one year
between famous and terrible years, a year
in which nothing at all happened—
Only a great hope, and his music,

and my sleeping with a girl in a quiet
room in Jerusalem's nights.
I had not seen him since then,
but hope for a better world has not
left his face to this day.

After that I bought myself
some nonkosher sausage
and two bagels and went home.
I ate and lay down on my bed
but the memory of my first love
came back to me
like the sudden sensation of falling
before sleep.

33

Listen, my old teacher: Life
is not deep as you taught us, history
and loves, Buber and Marx are
nothing but a thin skin of asphalt road
on this huge earth.

Oh, my teacher, the limit of toys is so near:
When a gun really kills and father is really dead.

And the limit of camouflage
which is also the limit of love:
Instead of a cannon there grows a real tree
and you become me
and I become you.

34

The door opened by mistake:
"You shouldn't be here now."

A thin whistle in the dark:
This was a young fig tree.

A slight despair lifted its head for a moment
like a watchdog and didn't even bark.

Rapists as in deep slumber in the forest
dreaming about real love.

"You shouldn't be here."
But here I am now.

Together we sailed to the sources of your madness:
a thundering waterfall. But in the morning
tranquil water.

35

In the garden at the white table
two dead men were sitting in the heat of day.
Above them, a branch moved slightly.
One of them pointed out things that never were,
the other spoke of a great love
with a special device to go on functioning
even after death.

It could be said they were
a cool and pleasant appearance
on this hot day, without sweat
and without voice. Only when they got up
I heard them like a ringing of porcelain
being removed from the table.

36

I'm like a leaf
knowing its limits,
not wanting to expand beyond
and not—
to become one with Nature
not to flow into the big world.

I'm so quiet now
I can't imagine
that I ever cried, even as a baby in pain.

My face is what is left
after they blasted it
and dug it for loves
like a stone quarry
now abandoned.

37

Karl Marx, cold and bitter one,
a man outside and a Jew in your grave in the foreign rain.
"Man lives by bread alone": Yourself
bread alone, lonely bread that you are,
round loaf from the last century,
a loaf rolling and tumbling the whole world
upside down.

Here I am on this winter day in Jerusalem
where tired Jews search the bodies of passersby:
collarbones, breast, belly, crotch: danger and love.
My skin still protects me against the rain,
but in one of my tears, if I'm still weeping then,
there will remain something of this water
pouring down now from heaven.

Karl Marx, with a beard like a sage.
Ritual slaughterer of history
so that it can be clean and kosher, according to the Law.
Look, I have put a lamp in my window
to make a field of light for myself.
I pay my rent on time. This too

is some kind of defense line, but directly
in front of it the enemy's armies
are lined up with rockets and thunder,
last battle and first death
and nothing after.

Look, my love caresses my breast
which is the hairy side of my emotions.

Karl Marx, the last drop
will always be a tear.

38

A weeping mouth and a laughing mouth
in terrible battle before a silent crowd.

Each gets hold of the mouth, tears and bites
the mouth, smashes it to shreds and bitter blood.

Till the weeping mouth surrenders and laughs,
till the laughing mouth surrenders and weeps.

39

My child dreamt about me in his sleep
while I was dreaming about my father, may he rest in
 peace.

You have a living father and I—a dead one.
You start and I want to finish.

I'm far away from emotion and feeling
as coal is far away from the forest it was.

Your time too will turn into thin thread
and the sweet "tick" will separate from the "tock."

The game begins: No looking out of the window!
And he who remembers last—he wins.

40

"But what have you done for your soul?"
I slept a lot and also loved a lot,
unlike the tree which loves just once a year.
What a forest of crazy trees I am!

And then, what am I? At most
a transmitter of childhood memories
with high poles above the landscape
from afar to afar.
And for the sake of this humming,
and a few sparks, all this hard labor,
all this running, all this pain?

Finally everything is made according to man's measurements,
a hand, a foot, a finger's length. Even
a high house is nothing but a man
on top of a man, on top of a man.

"But what have you done for your soul?"

41

The evening lies along the horizon and donates blood.
Flights of birds move up the sky like black mist.

Love is a reservoir of tenderness and care
like the hoarding of food for times of siege.

A little boy sits upright in his bed.
His kingdom is eternal kingdom.

People put a fence around their house,
so that their hope will not be in vain.

In a white and closed room
a woman decides to grow her hair long again.

The earth is turned up for the seed.
A secret military installation blossoms in the dark.

42

These words, like heaps of feathers
on the edge of Jerusalem, above the Valley of the Cross.
There, in my childhood, the women sat
plucking chickens.
These words fly now all over the world.
The rest is slaughtered, eaten,
digested, decayed, forgotten.

The hermaphrodite of time
who is neither day nor night
has wiped out this valley
with green well-groomed gardens.
Once experts of love used to come here
to perform their expertise
in the dry grass of summer nights.

That's how it started.
Since then—many words, many loves,
many flowers
bought for warm hands to hold
or to decorate tombs.

That's how it started
and I don't know how it will end.
But still, from beyond the valley,
from pain, and from distance
we shall forever go on calling out
to each other: "We'll change."

43

A song, a psalm, on Independence Day.
All of it so far off, but still remembered
like the echo of footsteps whose bodies
turned to dust of the desert long ago.
The sound of trumpets that I hear—
not for me anymore.
Even the warm breath inside the trumpets—
not for me anymore.
And the remembered dust has turned
into forgetting fields.

Builders and destroyers gather
in my house in the evening
to sit all night through on the balcony
watching the fireworks
which are the many-colored sighs of the Jewish people.

Come, let's not talk about the famous six million,
let's talk about just one of them—me:
I am a man like a dead mound.
But in each of my layers
something still moves.

44

The little park planted in memory of a boy
who fell in the war begins
to resemble him
as he was twenty-nine years ago.
Year by year they look more alike.
His old parents come almost daily
to sit on a bench
and look at him.

And every night the memory in the garden
hums like a little motor:
During the day you can't hear it.

45

On New Year's Day, next to a house being built,
a man vows not to do any wrong in it,
only to love in it.
Sins that were green in spring
have dried out in summer and now rustle and whisper.

So I washed my body and trimmed my fingernails—
the last favor
which a man does for himself
while he is still alive.

What is man? During the day
he breaks up into little words
what night has turned into a heavy lump.
What are we doing to each other?
What does a father do to his son?
What—a son to his father?

And nothing stands between
him and death
but a thin defense, like a battery
of excited lawyers,
a fence of words.

And he who uses people as handles, or as steps of a ladder,
will soon find himself

embracing a piece of wood
and holding a hand cut from its body
and wiping his tears
with a potsherd.

46

You carry the load of heavy buttocks,
but your eyes are clear.
Around your waist you wear a strong belt
which won't be able to protect you.

You are made of material that slows down
the process of joy and its pain.

I have already taught my penis
to say your name, like a clever bird.
You seem unimpressed by this,
you pretend not to hear it.
What else should I have done for you?

Now all that's left to me
is your name
which has become completely independent, like an animal:
It eats out of my hand and
lies down at night
curled up in my dark brain.

47

In the beginning there was great joy—
like the joy when two strangers meet.

Every night each one returns to his tunnel
to dig in it, alone.

In the morning there arrived the Non-Letter.

48

There came upon me a terrible longing
like people in an old photograph
who want to be back among the others
who are looking at them
in the good light of a lamp.

Here in this house I think
how love has turned into friendship
in the chemistry of our life.
I think about friendship which calms us for death
and how our lives are like single threads
without any hope of being rewoven
into another cloth.

Out of the desert
come muffled sounds,
dust prophesies dust, an airplane
fastens above our heads
the zipper of a huge bag of fate.

And the memory of a girl I once loved
moves along the valley tonight, like buses—
many lighted windows passing, many her-faces.

49

I am a man "planted beside streams of water,"
but I'm not "blessed be the man."
The desert is calm all around me, but there's no peace
 in me.
Two sons I have, one still small,
and whenever I see a child crying
I want to make another one
as if I hadn't got it right
and wanted to start afresh.
And my father is dead, and God is only one, like me.
And the Hill of Evil Counsel sails into the night
all covered with antennae up to heaven.

I'm a man planted beside streams of water,
but I can only weep it,
and sweat it, and urinate it
and spill it from my wounds—
all this water.

50

A song of friendship, while parting from a friend:
Now I shall extinguish my desert with your fat wet fields,
I shall drive deep into your green swamps
the burning sharp rocks of my country
like hot iron into eyes:
In hissing steam and in the white soothing vapor
again an old pain will unite us
and eternal joy will be on our heads.

Toward evening we stood once more together
in the field leaning to the river.
The smell of earth came up from beneath
and I said in my heart: Like dung on the soil,
good blessed dung and silence.

Goodbye, my friend, go back to your house
with your heavy steps. The light of sunset
will also light windows of houses
where nobody lives anymore.

51

To a friend who is a priest: With sad
and soft eyes you once more, as in ancient
times, swing the pampered thighbone
for a burned offering,
and smoke your private incense
in your half-clogged pipe.
You refuse to degrade yourself to
the caste of blessing priests in synagogue
with wailing voice and cramped
fingers like those of old women
or to receive alms at rituals of firstborn males.

Lacking beautiful ceremonious attire you
sit wrapped in the folds of your own fat
in the Turkish Bath among
crude and hairy laymen.
But you are still sensitive, almost allergic,
to dead corpses and cemeteries: Your hair
stands on end like the hair of a cat
when you pass near something dead.
In the pockets of your baggy trousers

which you take out of the iron locker
in the dressing room
a bunch of keys rings like
the little bells in the ancient Temple.

One of the keys is very old, and
has lost its house,
so my friend the priest
can whistle on it
to call back brilliant memories
like whistling a dog.

52

Jerusalem is a cradle city rocking me.
Whenever I wake up strange things happen to me
in the middle of the day, as though to someone
descending the stairs of his love's house
for the last time, with eyes still closed.
But my days force me to open my eyes and
to remember everyone passing me: Perhaps
he'll love me, perhaps he has planted a bomb
wrapped in nice paper like a present of love.
I observe all the weak spots in these stone houses,
the crack through which electricity enters,
the hole pierced for waterpipes,
the cunt for telephone wires to penetrate
and the mouths of sighs.

I am a Jerusalemite. Swimming pools with
their voices and noises are no part of my soul.
The dust is my conscious, the stone my subconscious,
and all my memories are closed courtyards
at summer's high noon.

53

At an archeological site
I saw fragments of precious vessels, well cleaned
and groomed and oiled and spoiled.
And beside it I saw a heap of discarded dust
which wasn't even good for thorns and thistles
   to grow on.

I asked: What is this gray dust which
has been pushed around and sifted
and tortured and then thrown away?

I answered in my heart: This dust
is people like us, who during their
lifetime lived separated from
copper and gold and marble stones
and all other precious things—
and they remained so in death.
We are this heap of dust, our
bodies, our souls, all the words
in our mouths, all hopes.

54

Evening hours of the soul
are upon me already in the morning.

Soft footsteps on lush grass, like hope
for something. Shoes always remain hard.

A little child stands motionless in the field
without knowing that he is thus eternal.

A man with two futures weeps in sudden fear,
a man empty of memories fills up his body, so he
 won't drift away.

A woman reads a letter at her window,
and doing so she changes beyond recognition.

A door opens and closes and opens.
Another remains closed: beyond it—silence.

55

A snare flies up from the ground
with outspread wings, this summer night.

A computer rolls his eyes upward
like a happy martyred saint.

Hoarse girls lure men
to their outings with hoarse voices.

In a lighted house sweet lovers tear
each other to quiet blood-dripping rags.

In the garages of the Kidron Valley
a black hearse is being repaired.

An orphaned father seats his little son on his knees
and sings him a lullaby about his sins.

The eyes of the sleepers are mines,
the first light of day will set them off.

56

In Talpiot* the floors are slowly sinking.
All the tiles are tired eyelids of the earth
wanting nothing but sleep.

The windows of the old house
have remained only for looking inside:
the final destiny of all windows.

Once I knew a woman here, with dark velvet eyes,
who used to keep saying: "Look
how the light falls."

Much have I loved her and
much has she spoiled sights of
landscapes and of love. But the light
she spoke of is still falling
and, unlike her, is
still unshattered.

* Talpiot—old suburb of modern Jerusalem.

57

The cemetery of Messilat Zion* in the mountains
of Jerusalem, toward evening:
a sudden relief after the narrow valley.
The people were born in India and came by air and by sea,
now buried here. Their graves in disarray,
each one pointing in a different direction,
like boats scattered after the storm has passed.

A blue wooden fence which can contain nothing.
Soft things cover the hard worlds in spring.
The Luf flower grows half hidden and
reminds me of deep and terrible things in my life.

I ask myself: Does salvation grow out
of all this? Does salvation grow
at all? And what are its seeds?

---

* Messilat Zion—a village in the mountains.

58

This man crossing the field was once
a Chief Rabbi in Africa. And I
used to be the chief lover in my house.
In spite of his age he is making
a new future for himself with
serious excursions and walks into
the Judaean mountains. He is learning.
He observes one wisdom piling up
stones for a wall and another wisdom
scattering them again all over the field.
He also observes a burnt field
and he knows by now that a burnt field
can never be burned again.
This too is some kind of hope and great peace.

All this is very well known,
like the blowing wind or
like Rachel mourning her children
in her grave.

59

Early in the morning
you lean against the wall of an old house.
After that you jump lightly
onto a bus with all the other jumpers.

With holy shoes like these
you go daily to work in an office
with a love dress like this,
to open and to close.

What protects you? Very thin
stockings up to your navel.

What supports this old house?
A memory supports it, till
you come to lean against it
next morning.

60

The day olive trees breathed deeply
and the hills learned again to dance like lambs
I saw my son's face when I was alone.
I was so alone that I saw.
Sleep in me, said the landscape, sleep, sleep.

I saw birds flying up and birds flying down
as when people leave you
and others come in their stead.

I saw men sitting in their homes
crying: "I want to go home!"
with the calm faces of men sitting
in their homes.

Sleep in me, said the landscape, sleep, sleep.

61

With open eyes as only the dead have
I travel. A lust to see other countries,
which filled me in my youth, has gone
without satisfaction.
Accustomed to travel, I stop at every door
and turn round, to see again
if I forgot something—
so I lengthen my stay.

And now I wait for the great happiness:
When my old mother will pace inside my brain
truly, in flesh and blood, with a stooped walk,
will pace, to and fro
from ear to ear, inside my brain—this
will be my great happiness.

62

Departure from a place where you had no love
includes the pain of all that did not happen
together with the longing for what will happen
   after you leave.

On my last evening I saw on the floor
of the balcony across the street
a small and exact square of light
bearing witness to great emotions
which have no limits.

And when I went early in the gray morning
to the railway station
many people were passing me
carrying lists of wonderful strange names
which I'll never come to know,
postmen, tax collectors, municipal clerks
and others. Perhaps angels.

63

When a man has been away from his homeland a long time,
his language becomes more and more precise
less and less impure,
like precise clouds of summer
on their blue background
which will never rain.

Thus, all those who were once lovers
still speak the language of love, sterile
and clear, never changing, and never
getting any response.

But I, who have stayed here, dirty my mouth
and my lips and my tongue.
In my words there is garbage of soul
and refuse of lust and dust and sweat.
Even the water I drink in this dry land,
between screams and memories of love,
is urine recycled back to me
through complicated circuits.

64

I love these people in their strong house
in the high North. From their window
you can see ships on their proud voyage
to an even farther North.
And whatever does not pass this window
does not exist.

Many islands, and not one memory.
The forests stand in everlasting rains,
the fat fern fronds are the only clue
to ancient happenings which were better forgotten.
And in the clearing, wet leaves in the mud
are a bed for burning love, with white steam.

"I'm the soul of this landscape," said
the woman. And so said another one,
and another, and another.

65

The house, in which I had many thoughts
when I was young, fell to pieces.
And so my thoughts are at large in the world and
 endanger me now.

Therefore I roam about a lot and change houses
so they won't find me.
Between two questions,
Has he arrived? and, Is he still here?
I always slip away, to new places.

The way of all flesh I'll go: hunted,
caught, slaughtered, sold even before
being killed, made kosher with bitter salt,
cut and tortured,
a strange life I have
and a strange death too
and a strange grave
with engraving mistakes
on the headstone.

66

Late in life I came to you
filtered through many doors
reduced by stairs
till almost nothing remained of me.

You are such a surprised woman
living with half courage,
a wild woman wearing spectacles—
those elegant reins of your eyes.

"Things like to get lost and be
found again by others. Only
human beings love to find themselves,"
you said.

After that you broke your whole face
into two equal profiles: one
for the far distance, the other for me—
as a souvenir. And you went.

67

We walked together, you and I,
like Abraham and his son Isaac.
But although we were a man and a woman,
and although we did not go to the sacrifice,
the knowledge of things still to happen
and the ignorance of what will befall
were close together, like lovers.

After that jaws of suitcases gaped open
and it turned out that what
we thought would be a few days of separation
became forever.

But since then there have remained between us
signs and special marks
like those exchanged by people who don't know each other
when they plan
to meet in places where they have never been.

68

Small and fragile you stand in the rain,
a small target for raindrops in winter
and for the dust in summer
and also for fragments of bombs all year round.
Your belly is weak, unlike the
taut flat skin of a drum.
Yours is the softness of the third generation.
Your grandfather, the pioneer, dried swamps.
But the revenge of those swamps falls on you,
filling you with sucking madness,
boiling and babbling in many colors.

What will you do now? You'll collect
loves like stamps. Some of them are duplicates
and some are damaged. No one will trade with you.
Your mother's curse crouches at your side
like an exotic bird. You resemble it.

Your room stays empty. But every night
your bed is made with a clean sheet.
That's hell's punishment for your bed:
no one sleeping in it, without
wrinkles, without a stain,
like the cursed sky in summer.

69

My son, in whose face there is already a sign
of eagle—
like a daring prefix to your life,
let me kiss you once more while you still love it,
softly, like this.
Before you become a hairy Esau of open fields
be for a little while
soft-skinned Jacob for my blind hands.

Your brain is well packed in your skull,
efficiently folded for life. Had it stayed
spread out you might have been happier,
a large sheet of happiness without memory.

I'm on my way from believing in God
and you're on your way toward it: This too
is a meeting point of a father and a son.

It's evening now. The earthball is cooling,
clouds that have never lain with a woman
pass overhead in the sky, the desert
starts breathing into our ears,
and all the generations
squeeze a bar mitzvah for you.

70

In this valley which many waters
carved out in endless years
so that the light breeze may now
pass through it to cool my forehead,
I think about you. From the hills I hear
voices of men and machines wrecking and building.

And there are loves which cannot
be moved to another place.
They must die at their place and in their time
like an old clumsy piece of furniture
that's destroyed together with
the house in which it stands.

But this valley is a hope
of starting afresh without having to die first,
of loving without forgetting the other love,
of being like the breeze
that passes through it now
without being destined for it.

71

"He left two sons," that's
what they say about someone
who died. Sometimes he is still alive.

The echo of a great love is like
the echo of a huge dog's barking
in an empty Jerusalem house
marked for demolition.

72

My ex-pupil has become a policewoman.
There she is, standing at the crossroads in town:
She opens a box made of metal,
like a box of perfumes and cosmetics,
and changes the colors of the traffic lights
   according to her mood.

Her eyes are a mixture of green, red and yellow.
Her hair is cut very short, like that of fresh street urchins.
In her high black shoes she leans against the box.
Her skirt is short and tight. I don't even dare
to imagine all the terrible glory at the upper
end of all this golden tan.

I don't understand anymore. I'm already lost.
When I walk the street whole legions
of young men and young women are
thrown against me in ever-growing waves.
They seem to have endless reserves.
And my pupil, the policewoman,
is unable to stop them:
She even joins them!

73

Such a male on a bald mountain in Jerusalem,
a scream pries open his mouth,
a wind tears at his cheeks and reins him in
like a bit in the mouth of an animal.

The message of his love: "Be fruitful and multiply"
is a messy business like sticky sweets
on a child's fingers—and attracts flies.
Or like a half-empty tube of shaving cream
crusted and split.
The threats of his love: On your back!
You with all your legs and trembling antennae!
Just wait, I'll drive it deep into you,
as far as your great grandchildren.
And she'll answer him: They will
bite you deep inside me,
they'll be a generation of tough
rodents, those last offspring!

"But a man is not a horse," said the old
cobbler while he was widening and softening
my new and hard shoes.
And suddenly I wept, because of so much
love being poured over me.

74

So I find myself always on the run
from blows and from pain,
from sweaty hands and from hard hits.
Most of my life in Jerusalem, a bad place
to evade all these. All my wars took
place in deserts among hard stones and sharp wounding
 gravel.
I never had the luck to have a war
in a cool green forest
or in a wavy battle at sea.

And so I am on the run, evasive like
a pathetic dancer amid hurled stones
and falling shells, between strong
hands and outstretched arms,
a very clumsy and heavily loaded
man I am on the run,
my whole body loaded down from head to toe,
on my shoulder a rifle, around my belly
an ammunition belt, on my head
heavy guilt, my feet in shoe-cages,
on my back the heavy yoke of family care,

and even my knees, moving up and down,
activate a terrible time-motor.

Only my penis is still free and happy,
no good for sword fights and no good
for any work, or even for hanging things on,
or for digging trenches.
Praise be to God that it is so. Even onto
God I've loaded praise.

And so, much too heavy, I'm
on the run till the last pain
causes me no more pain.

75

A bird at dawn is singing
with too strong a voice
prophesying a day of dry hot winds.

At noon the shutters are pulled down
against the burning sun.
Then my soul makes love to me
from behind, all along my back
and I'm unable to return
to work because of all this pleasure.

Toward evening, the so-called Present Situation
lifts itself up from the people and
hangs up there, in one piece, like a high canopy,
and the quantity
of all the water in the world is turned
into the quality
of one tear in the eye.

76

On the wall of a house on which
bricks were painted I saw
visions of God.

A sleepless night which makes pain in the heads of others
made flowers opening in my brain.

And he who was lost like a dog
will be found like a man and come back.

Love is not the last room:
There are others along
the long corridor that has no end.

77

My God, the soul
you gave me
is smoke—
from never-ending burnings
of memories of love.

The minute we are born
we start burning them
and so on
until the smoke
dies, like smoke.

78

Here on the ancient beach of Tantura I sit
in the sand with my sons and my sons' sons not yet born.
But they are assembled with me in my crouched squatting.
The happiness of the water equals the happiness of heaven.
And the waves' foam penetrates my mind and becomes
   clear there.

And my past's future is here and now in my rest.
I see children playing in the sand:
The happy ones always destroy and
the sad ones build again.
But the voices of both are stronger
than the sound of the breaking waves.

There on that hillock beside the railway tracks
an old concrete pillbox still stands.
Thorns cover it. Its iron died long ago,
but its shooting slits have become
real eyes, sometimes seeing
and sometimes weeping thin sand.

There I stood in the summer of 1942
facing the sea, guarding against the enemy
to protect the continuation of my life
to reach until this moment.
New enemies come now from the east,
but the same wind still nestles
in sleepless reddened eyes.

79

Now all the lifeguards have left for their homes.
The bay is closed and all of the
sun's last light is concentrated
in a fragment of glass,
like all life in the breaking eye of the dying.

A clean washed board is saved
from the fate of becoming furniture.
Half an apple and half a footprint
in the sand try to become together
a new whole thing.
A blackened box looks like a man asleep or dead.
But even God stopped here and did
not approach it to know the truth.
The one and only mistake and the
one and only right thing we do
both bring peace to a man's mind.
The balance sheets of good and bad
are being opened and pour slowly
into the tranquil world.

In the dim light of dusk, by the
rock pool, a few young people still

warm themselves with emotions
I once had in this place.
Inside the water the green stone
looks like it's dancing with the dead
fish in rippling waves.
A girl's face emerges from diving
with eyelashes like rays of the sun
resurrected for the night.

80

So I went down to the ancient harbor: Deeds
of human beings bring the sea closer,
other deeds push it farther away.
How can the sea know what they want, which pier clasps
as in love, and which pier rejects?

In the shallow water lies a Roman column.
But this is not its final place. Even if they
take it from here and set it in a museum
with a small explanation, even that will
not be its final place: It will go on falling
through floors and strata and other times.

But now a breeze blowing through the tamarisks
fans a last red glow in the cheeks of those sitting there
like embers of a dying bonfire. After that, night
   and whiteness.
The salt eats everything and I eat
salt, till it eats me too.
And what was given to me was again taken
from me and again given, and what was thirsty
has since quenched its thirst,
and what was quenched has found rest in death.